Snow for Christmas

ILLUSTRATED BY GILL GUILE
WRITTEN BY DIANE JACKMAN

Brimax Books · Newmarket · England

"Will it snow this Christmas?"
Polly asked her mother.
"I've never seen snow,"
said Sam. "Except in pictures."
"We'll have to wait and see if
Mother Goose shakes her
feathers," said his mother.
"That's what my Grandma used
to say to me when it snowed –
Mother Goose is shaking her
feathers again."
"That's silly," said Sam.
Mother smiled. "Is it?"

On Christmas Eve, Polly and Sam went to bed early. They hung their stockings up ready for Santa Claus. Soon they were fast asleep. Suddenly, Polly woke up. "Sam! I can hear a noise!" She crept to the window, lifted the curtain and peeped out into the darkness.

Polly could hardly believe her eyes. Outside was a goose. Not an ordinary goose like the ones in Farmer Smith's field, this goose wore a green bonnet and a red shawl. She was searching for something in the bushes. "Wake up, Sam!" cried Polly. Sam stirred and opened one eye. "It's Mother Goose," said Polly.

“Don’t be silly,” grumbled Sam. “That was just a story. You’ve been dreaming.”
“No I have not!” said Polly. “She’s out there and she looks exactly like Mother Goose in my storybook.”
“I suppose she’s carrying a sack of feathers to shake over us,” said Sam with a yawn. But he still went to the window to have a look.

"Whatever shall I do?" Mother Goose was saying. "Where can it be?" She lifted the lid of the rain barrel and looked inside. "I'm sure I left it here. There'll be no snow for Christmas now."
Polly opened the bedroom window and called, "Can we help, Mother Goose?"

The sound of Polly's voice above her head made Mother Goose squawk in alarm. "How you startled me! I've lost my sack of feathers," she explained. "I must find it or there'll be no snow for Christmas." Polly and Sam quickly dressed and ran downstairs to help Mother Goose in her search.

Polly searched in the woodshed. She found sacks of logs and long-legged spiders. Sam searched in the greenhouse. He found sacks of potatoes and dusty flowerpots. Mother Goose searched in the barn. She found sacks of corn and squeaking mice. Nobody found a sack of feathers.

"When did you last have your sack?" asked Sam.
"Yesterday," said Mother Goose, "when I passed your house. I stopped to talk to a friend. Then I went on, leaving the feathers behind."
"Someone else must have found it," said Polly. "There are only two houses along this road. Ours and Mrs Crackle's."
"Let's ask Mrs Crackle," said Sam.

They found Mrs Crackle sitting beside a blazing fire. "Come in," she said. "It's cold enough for snow."
"We shan't have any snow," said Sam.
"Not unless Mother Goose finds her sack of feathers," said Polly.
"Sack of feathers you say," said Mrs Crackle, beginning to smile. "I think I can help you."

Mrs Crackle led the way to a cupboard under the stairs. "The sack of feathers was by the road," she said. "No one came to collect it and the feathers were so clean and white, I decided to make myself a new feather quilt. But someone else had the same idea. Look!" Mrs Crackle shone a lamp into the dark cupboard.

There was Mother Goose's sack, and there was Mrs Crackle's ginger cat, Miranda, curled up in the soft feathers with five ginger kittens. "I can't disturb the kittens," said Mother Goose. "Don't worry," said Mrs Crackle. "We'll think of something."

Polly, Sam and Mother Goose sat down to think. Before they had even one idea, the door opened and in padded Miranda, carrying a kitten in her mouth. She dropped him gently on the hearth-rug. Backwards and forwards she went until all five kittens lay in a furry heap, purring happily, Miranda beside them.

Stopping only long enough to thank everyone and take her sack of feathers, Mother Goose flapped her wings and flew away. As Polly and Sam waved goodbye, a handful of soft, white feathers drifted down and the first snowflakes they had ever seen began to fall. "Snow for Christmas!" shouted Sam. "Thank you, Mother Goose!" said Polly.

Say these words again.

snow
bonnet
feathers
kitten
curtain
searching
yawn
lost
quickly
greenhouse
squeaking
barn
quilt
lamp